How To Tune

With Musical Precision

as a

Complete Instrument

For Drummers, Drum Techs, Music Teachers

Recording Engineers & Producers

The Well-Tempered Drum Kit

First Edition

George Kiapos

ISBN-13: 978-0692360095
ISBN-10: 0692360093

Printed in the United States of America.

George Kiapos

Dedicated to my beautiful children
Marco & Manon

Table of Contents

Introduction

What amazes me is that I have yet to find a drum tuning system that has explained what I am about to share. I've run across some drum techs who understand part of what I'm about to explain. However, I haven't seen, heard or read anyone who explains the bigger picture about drum tuning. This is what I will teach you. You will discover that it is quite simple. There is one simple relationship to know. However, the possibilities are exponential.

Before I begin to get into the details, the first thing that is so often overlooked is that a drum kit makes up a complete instrument. In the way that I will teach you how to tune drums, I will show you that an entire drum set is no different, in theory, than a piano, a guitar, or any other tunable instrument. And, guitars, pianos, etc., follow a specific protocol and technique that allow them to be "in tune." Drums are no different. It's important to realize that a piano is a percussion instrument -- just like a drum set. Both are completely capable of producing notes that work in a musical relationship to what's being played. Rather than think about each individual drum as an independent component, I want you to consider your entire drum set as a complete instrument.

I have studied countless methods by people who have somehow dismissed this very critical aspect of drum tuning. I've also read some of the top selling books on how to tune drums. They all share the basic principals of how to mount, seat and bring the heads to a certain pitch. However, they neglect to inform us how to arrive at a specific and desired pitch, or note. They also neglect to inform us how to tune our drums to notes that resonate musically with the rest of the drums. As passionate and knowledgable as these respectable people are -- and want to share what they know -- they all fail to address drum tuning from the perspective that I am going to share. I don't know why this perspective has been overlooked so often by even some of the world's most renown players, technicians, or otherwise. I am certain that their intentions are all honorable. I will show you how you can tune your drums as a unified and cohesive musical instrument, and have complete control as to how you can arrive at doing so. Furthermore, the method that I will teach you works on any kind of shell -- maple, birch, poplar, hybrids, metal, acrylic, etc. The method also works on any brand of drum head -- Remo, Evans, Acquarian, etc., -- coated or clear, ported or not.

*Note: *Quality drum heads as mentioned above play an important role in overall drum tone.*

Chapter One

Sweet Spots

Many drum enthusiasts talk about a drum shell's fundamental note as produced by the factory, or finding a "sweet spot," or "tuning a drum to itself," from which the drum apparently sounds "best." This may all be true. But, think of the following: A guitar's D string's "sweet spot" is the note D-3, which is 146.8 Hz. The same goes for a piano. A piano's middle C's "sweet spot" is C-4, which is 261.6 Hz.

Every tunable instrument is dependent upon the appropriate overall tuning that enables it to sound and perform at its best potential. There's no difference with the drum kit.

When a drummer or technician focuses too much on one particular drum, the bigger picture is lost. Trying to find such sweet spots is often hit or miss, and one particular drum's "perfect" tuning may not necessarily be in "tune" with another. Because of this, unwanted overtones can often clash between several of the drums configured in the kit. This is often the result of having no real rationale behind the overall tuning of the drums as a unified instrument – like 88 keys on a piano.

What I will show you is that an entire drum kit can have a "collective sweet spot" comprised of individual sweet spots when tuned in compliance with basic musical relationships.

Chapter Two

Frequencies

Notes and their representative frequencies -- measured in Hertz (Hz) -- are the most fundamental aspect of tuning any instrument. Any electronic and digital tuning device relies entirely upon matching the correct frequencies in Hz to the desired note being tuned. Whether or not anyone realizes this, it's that simple. A guitar player doesn't have to understand frequencies in Hertz to know that his strings are in tune because the green light goes on in the little gadget clipped on to his headstock. This is truly a convenience, and an expediter that allows a musician to play in tune.

You don't necessarily have to know all the acoustical mechanics involved when arriving at a note. However, recording engineers and savvy music producers already have a strong knowledge base involving frequency principals, especially in the EQ process of recording and mixing.

With respect to drums, it's just as important to be "in tune" as it is with other instruments. This is so often misunderstood. Many drummers tend to think that they've somehow stumbled upon certain drum tunings that they trust works best for them. There's nothing wrong with this. And, in many cases these self arrived at tuning methods do work for their purposes. However, this "experimental" process is usually intuitive -- without necessarily corresponding to fundamental musical relationships.

I understand all too well that drummers are often a rogue breed among musicians. They are the time keepers and focus primarily more on being the heart beat that drives the tempo. Furthermore, many drummers don't pay too much attention to their overall drum sound, and often leave this task up to the drum technician, or music producer. Getting that fat or cracky snare sound, responsive tom attack and the perfect thump in the kick drum usually seem to be of primary concern.

However, the more a drummer has a grip on having the tools to create virtually whatever sound one wants their kit to have -- with formulated precision -- the more valuable he, or she may be with their contribution to the musical aspect of what they're playing. All of the above can be achieved with what is provided in the information that I'm about to share.

Music theory is helpful, but not necessarily essential to learn and understand what I will teach you. Obviously, the more you already know about music, the better. Yet, sticking to a few basic principals is all you need. Understanding only the very basics of frequencies is more valuable than you might imagine.

Chapter Three

Dynamic Range

I am specifically avoiding most of the rudimentary information involved with mounting and seating a drum head and systematically tightening the lugs to arrive at a desired pitch. There are many excellent free video tutorials available on YouTube that present thorough and detailed information concerning these basics. A seasoned drummer and drum tech know these procedures inside out. However, it is from that very point of tensioning the drum heads where I will explain how to tune your drums to any desired note you wish -- within each drum's basic dynamic range.

Drums are inherently limited to tuning range based on shell size. The process that I will show you will give you a greater understanding to this condition. This knowledge will not slow anything down in the tuning process. It will most likely take no longer than what you're already doing when you tune your drums the way you currently do. The only difference is that I will direct you as to how you can arrive at specific pitches -- within each drum shell's range -- that can help, and improve your overall drum sound.

What I am providing in the later pages of the book will refer to Frequency Charts (Chapter 13). One will be tabled according to all the notes covering all the octaves, another will be illustrated on an 88 key piano, while a third will be a bar graph showing tunable ranges covering seven of the most common drum shell diameters. All will give the identical information, yet from different visual contexts. What these charts will provide is an overall reference which may serve as a guide to how you may wish to tune your drums based on individual notes and their relative frequencies. The last chart will show you that the dynamic range in overall drum tuning – with respect to FUNDAMENTAL NOTES – spans just over two octaves.

Chapter Four

Tuning Devices

Please note that electronic tuning devices can be extremely helpful if your ears aren't sensitive enough to determine the finer nuances of discerning exact frequencies. Although, I strongly suggest trusting your ears first. The use of a musician's ears is how instruments have been tuned throughout history prior to the advent of such devices, notwithstanding the tuning fork. If you prefer using a device, like Tune Bot ®, or Drumtune PRO ®, etc., by all means do so. However, with a sensitive ear, a guitar, piano, or any virtual instrument capable of producing notes in a couple of octave range can enable you to arrive at the same results — and, increase your ears sensitivity.

Drums can easily get slightly out of tune not long after you've tuned them -- even if you use the most sophisticated devices. This happens with virtually all tunable instruments. And, it is more likely than not to happen with drums. This is due to the fact that many lugs are required to bring a drum into tune. An example is that a 12" tom with 6 lugs on both batter and resonant heads has 12 overall lugs to bring the drum into tune. A slight variance in tension of just one lug can render the drum out of tune. However, this simple reality reminds us that nothing is perfect. So, getting as close as you can is generally what drummers have to deal with -- whether or not an electronic tuning device is used.

I do not recommend drum dials. No matter how close you may want to reach perfect and even tension, you never will when it boils down to tuning each lug to the same pitch. There will always be slight differences in lug tension. It's not the equal tension that's important as much as it is the equal tuning of each lug. Although, we always want to be *as close* to equal tension as possible.

Chapter Five

Harmonic Resonance

Without getting into unnecessary and complicated details, harmonic resonance basically deals with frequencies that are in harmonic multiples, and sympathetic to one another. There is a specific relationship in frequencies that work best with others. This is a natural law that cannot be denied. It's like God telling us, *"These sets of frequencies always work best together."* From a musical standpoint, there are various combinations of this universal principal.

Tuning your instrument is the most critical aspect of how your instrument sounds and plays. We already know that tensioning the drum heads with a drum key is the way to tune drums. However, I will give you the reasons WHY you need to tighten your lug tension rods to a certain pitch -- on **both** batter and resonant heads. There is a definite and very practical reason that fulfills an overall target of attaining musical resonance among the basic drum set configurations. No matter what level you're at as a player, at least your drums will sound good. How you play is up to your own skill level.

In short order, I will show you how to tune each individual drum in perfect harmonic resonance to a fundamental note. Afterwards, I will also show you how to tune the entire kit in harmonic resonance to all the other drums. I will later provide diagrams of basic 4 piece, 5 piece and 6 piece drum kits. The 5 piece kit can be either two up and one down, or one up and two down. This will be later illustrated in comprehensive diagrams (Chapter 15).

The purpose of tuning your drums in harmonic resonance has little to do with trying to tune your drums to a specific song or key. However, in the studio, this can be easily achieved if so desired. More importantly, its purpose is to create an overall "marriage" of how your drums sound when played together as a unit, or "complete instrument." The choice of tuning your entire drum kit as a cohesive harmonic instrument is entirely up to you. If you choose not to do this, I will at the very least show you how you can tune every one of your drums to a desired fundamental note -- within the drum shell range -- with complete precision and ease.

Before we actually get started, it's important for you to know that the system used to tune each specific drum works for each and every drum. You don't have to treat your snare drum any differently than your floor tom in terms of *how* you are tuning (other than separating your snare wires with a drum stick). The method for each drum is identical. So, let's get started.

Chapter Six

Resonant & Batter Head Relationships

The most important fundamental element to drum tuning is understanding the dynamic relationship between the bottom, or Resonant (Reso) Head, and the top, or Batter Head. What I am about to explain works 100% of the time, every time, on any drum in your kit. I call it *musical magic.* All you need is your ear, and a simple reference device, or instrument that plays simple notes.

I began doing this using only an acoustic guitar. But, any instrument or device -- including a virtual piano -- that plays all the notes with sharps and flats within a couple of octaves will work just fine.

It's widely known among drum professionals and technicians that tuning the bottom/reso head to a higher pitch than the top/batter head yields perhaps the most popular and preferred tone among drummers. This may be arguable. Yet, I can suggest that this method may be the most commonly used. Jeff Ocheltree mentions this in his DVD *"Trust Your Ears"* when demonstrating how John Bonham tuned his drums. Bonham's technique was inspired by many of the great big band drummers. It's highly likely that Gene Krupa, Buddy Rich, Louis Belson and so many others employed this reso to batter head relationship. Bonham understood that these masters knew what they were doing. In turn, he became among the icons from which he emulated.

In addition to any great drummer's skill level, much of what makes us appreciate what they do is also largely based on the sounds produced by their drum sets. How they tune their drums is every bit important as how they play their drums.

Chapter Seven

Important Basics before Tuning

The only mechanical processes in reference to drum tuning are the following basic principals that nearly every drummer already knows. However, they're well worth repeating as to arrive at the process I'm going to show you:

1. When tuning either head, mute the opposite head by placing the "down" side of the drum on a padded surface that comes into contact with the drum head facing down. (A drum throne, a lazy susan turntable with a muting pad, or a coffee table with some kind of muting pad. They all work).

2. Always tune the lugs in an opposing pattern (like changing a car tire). Patterns will vary according to the number of lugs on a drum (see diagram below). Use two drum keys at opposite ends, if possible. Do this until you begin to get *close* to the desired pitch. Afterwards, you may tune only the lugs that need to be adjusted to the desired pitch in any sequence necessary.

3. Use your finger to tap the drum head when you can. I find that there is a closer connection to the tuning process when we involve our own sense of touch. Otherwise, use the drum key to gently tap the drum head. Make sure that you tap about an inch away from the bearing edge at each corresponding lug.

When you reach your desired pitch/frequency on each lug, you'll notice that the transient frequencies will become more consistent as well. And, overtones will become less noticeable. Usually, those with more sensitive hearing can discern this. I've provided a diagram to illustrate typical lug tuning sequences according to lug patterns.

Lastly, always tune up to a pitch — like tuning a guitar string. Tuning up helps to lock the pitch into place. Conversely, tuning down has a tendency to go flat.

Lug Tuning Pattern Diagram

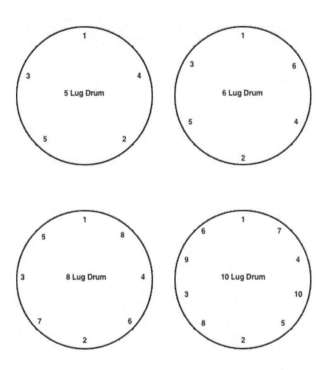

Chapter Eight

The Magic of Fourths
Tuning Your Reso Head Higher

It is already well known that perfect fourths work extremely well in this application. In this relationship between the bottom and top heads, **the bottom/reso head must be tuned a perfect fourth higher than the top/batter head.** A simple example of this is to tune the bottom/reso head to an "A" note, and tune the top/batter head to an "E" note.

Here's where the *formula* comes in. When striving to tune your drum to a specific note, understand the following: In this application, whatever note you tune your bottom/reso head to will become the FUNDAMENTAL NOTE of the drum, as long as the top/batter head is a perfect fourth lower in the scale. So, to tune a rack tom to the fundamental note of A (110 Hz), simply tune the bottom/reso head to A (220 Hz) AND the top/batter head to E (164.81 Hz). When you mount your tom and strike the top/batter head, the fundamental note of the drum will ALWAYS be A (110 Hz, A - 2 on the piano). Always. Every time. Without fail.

*Note: While tapping the drum heads in the tuning phase, the frequencies of both reso and batter heads will be one octave higher in range. This results from two reasons:

1) *The drum head is being tapped closer to the bearing edge, which creates a higher frequency response.*

2) *When you mute the opposite drum head, no resonance is produced from that opposing head. This occurs on both reso and batter heads as long as their opposite heads are muted. As mentioned, when **un-muted**, the fundamental reso head note will be produced from **both** reso and batter heads: A full octave lower than the reso head – while both frequencies of each head are maintained as tuned in their respective octaves.*

I know of NO OTHER WAY of tuning drums with relationships between reso and batter heads that can produce this formula with pure consistency and accuracy.

Important Note:

An electronic tuning device may be able to determine reso and batter head frequencies independently. However, the device may not be able to distinguish between reso and batter head frequencies if used to "read" the drum's FUNDAMENTAL NOTE. The best way to know your fundamental note is to listen to it. And, it will most definitely be one octave lower than the reso head, when the reso head is tuned a fourth higher than the batter head. It would be more accurate to compare the fundamental note to that of a tuned instrument.

Chapter Nine

Tuning the Batter Head Higher

Using the same relationship in perfect fourths in reverse produces the same pitch result, but with exceptions. Using the "fourths" principal, when the top/batter head is tuned to A (220 Hz), and the bottom/reso head is tuned to E (164.81 Hz), the fundamental note of the drum is still A (110 Hz). The fundamental note is *always* the higher pitch within this relationship of fourths. This may be because the lower frequency resonates off of the higher frequency in a sympathetic relationship of natural harmonics. However, the tone of the drum *varies drastically*.

With the reso head being at the lower pitch, there are many more transient frequencies heard. It's my belief that having a higher pitched, and respectively tighter resonant head plays an important role in the sound dynamic of drums. With the batter head being lower, the movement of air from the stick attack responds much faster in frequency when bouncing off a tighter surface below.

Conversely, when the batter head is tighter, and the reso head is looser, frequency vibration moving in the air space between drum heads is slowed down, and absorbed by the lower tuned resonant head. Think of a trampoline. If the trampoline is looser, the person bouncing moves deeper into the net, and consequently slower. If the net is tighter, then the person bounces a little more shallow into the net and consequently faster. This is the same dynamic that occurs from the air movement following the stick attack from the batter head. The reso head is like the trampoline net.

With the batter head being tighter, it's my observation that the resulting transient notes are somehow "confused" in the delayed reaction when bouncing off the looser reso head in this dynamic relationship. To my ears, the sound is muddy. And, I don't have a scientific explanation. All I know is that the drum sounds much fuller, rounder, brighter and with better response when the reso head is tuned *higher* than the batter head in this relationship of fourths.

This is perhaps why so many people opt to tune their resonant heads higher than their batter heads -- whether or not tuned in fourths. This reason may very well adhere to a natural law in acoustical dynamics that the musician can intuitively hear and feel. After all, musician's ears are trained to be sensitive to sound frequencies.

Chapter Ten

Tuning Both Heads to the Same Pitch

One would think that if you tuned both the reso and batter heads on your 12" tom equally to A (220 Hz), your drum would play the fundamental note of A (220 Hz). But, IT DOESN'T. Instead, this equal tuning of the heads results in C# (138.59 Hz). This is four and a half steps down the scale from the equally tuned heads. Furthermore, if I tune both reso and batter heads to G (196 Hz), the resulting fundamental note of the drum becomes Bb (116.54 Hz). This difference is five and a half steps down the scale from the equally tuned heads.

You can see that there is no consistent relationship of determining a fundamental note when both heads are tuned equally. This is why tuning top and bottom heads to the same pitch is a "hit or miss" proposition. You have little control over your entire drum kit. So, you may ask yourself why some of our world's greatest drummers opted to tune their reso heads higher in pitch than their batter heads? Most likely because it works better. And, in my opinion, the drums sound better. There's generally more attack and slightly less resonance. This is why older drum manufacturers opted to incorporate mufflers on the drums, or why products like Moongel ® exist – and why drummers often use folded tape on their drum heads. They serve to reduce too much natural resonance that is often produced by a drum.

Chapter Eleven

Tuning Empowerment

What I've just showed you may be more empowering than you realize. What you now know so far, you have complete control on how to tune each and every one of your drums in your kit to a desired note -- within each drum shell's inherent dynamic range. I will provide these basic dynamic ranges in the next chapter. With this valuable knowledge, you can also create a symmetrical harmonic relationship throughout your entire drum kit. There is no" hit or miss." It's all within your reach -- taking no longer than it would to tune your drums the way you've been doing so already. Yet, now, you are in the driver's seat with concern to how you want your drums to sound.

The potential that opens up from this offers a host of possibilities. Command over your drums tuning potentials have now become enormous. You will clearly see this illustrated -- all according to musical principals -- when you begin to review the drum diagrams I've provided in Chapter 15.

Chapter Twelve

Basic Dynamic Tuning Ranges

It's important to note that depending on the size of the drum shell, there is an inherent built in dynamic range of frequencies that can work. For the sake of simplicity, I've created a **basic** list of typical frequencies that range and generally apply to specific drum shell sizes. Manufacturer's and shell material may vary within the frequency range presented. It's best to test your own drum shells and specifically determine their dynamic tuning ranges.

The chart on the next page will break down all seven basic drum shell sizes, beginning with the 14" Snare drum, followed by 10" - 12" - 13" - 14" - 16" Toms, and a 22" Kick drum. This **Table** provides an example of drum shell size to frequency range relationships. The notes in **bold** are usually the most commonly tuned frequencies per drum shell size. It's a good idea to become familiar with these relationships.

The Table will also provide tuning suggestions for achieving classic snare tones. It's been my experience that certain "go to" snare tunings can easily render basic variations ranging from crisp and cracky to thick and fat. With the notes and frequencies provided, these results are easily achieved.

Table of Typical Drum Shell Dynamic Tuning Range

size	low	high	low – high range
10" Tom	C-3 (130.80 Hz)	G-3 (196.00 Hz)	C-3,C#-3,**D-3,Eb-3,E-3,F-3**,F#-3,G-3
12" Tom	G#-2 (103.80 Hz)	Eb-3 (155.56 Hz)	G#-2, **A-2,Bb-2,B-2,C-3,C#-3**,D-3,Eb-3
13" Tom	F#-2 (92.50 Hz)	C#-3 (138.60 Hz)	F#-2,G-2,**G#-2,A-2,Bb-2,B-2**,C-3,C#-3
14" Tom	Eb-2 (77.78 Hz)	Bb-2 (116.5 Hz)	Eb-2,**E-2,F-2,F#-2,G-2**,G#-2,A-2,Bb-2,B-2
16" Tom	Bb-1 (58.27 Hz)	F-2 (87.31 Hz)	Bb-1,B-1,**C-2,C#-2,D-2,Eb-2,E-2**,F-2,F#-2

5 x 14" Snare

    Eb-3 (155.6 Hz)   B-3 (246.90 Hz)   Eb-3,F-3,**F#-3,G-3,G#-3,A-3,Bb-3**,B-3

Note: FAT snare sounds work well in the ± "F-3" range.

                FAT – MED in the "G-3" range.

                TIGHT & CRACKY in the ± "B-3" range.

                *Overall snare dynamic range also varies in shell depth.

16" x 22" Kick

    F-1 (43.65 Hz)   C-2 (65.41 Hz)   F-1,F#-1,**G-1,G#-1,A-1,Bb-1,B-1**,C-2,C#-2,D-2

Note: Smaller to Larger Kick drums can vary in dynamic range.

                Figure ± 1-1/2 to 2 steps either way for each incremental difference in size.

Note: Jazz tunings sometimes push the envelop toward the higher end of the shell's range.

The following examples will show exactly note to frequency relationships as illustrated with: Notes & Frequency Chart, Piano Keyboard Frequency Chart, and Bar Chart - Notes & Frequencies.

Chapter Thirteen

Notes & Frequency Charts

Three Basic Frequency Charts are hereby provided for quick reference. These note to frequency relationships can easily be used along with electronic tuning devices to arrive at specific and desired pitches that you may choose to tune your drums. Although the first Table lists virtually all the notes, overall drum tuning only covers a span of a little over two octaves.

It's important to become somewhat familiar with frequencies and their respective notes that fall within the F-1 (43.65 Hz) and B-3 (246.9 Hz) range. These notes and frequencies generally cover all the drum sizes listed in the previous chapter ranging from high and cracky snare tunings to low and thumping kick tunings. Anything in between generally falls within the Toms, varying from 10" to 16."

*Note: *Consider that an 18" floor tom, or bass drum will fall between a 16" Tom and a 22" kick drum. Also, diameter is the critical dimension for dynamic tuning range, and not shell depth.*

Although far too many notes than needed are provided in the following tables, take the time to briefly review them. It's always a good idea to familiarize yourself with how musical notes are nothing more than specific sonic vibrations that resonate according to natural physical laws in the universe.

Frequency Tables

	C	C#	D	Eb	E	F	F#	G	G#	A	Bb	B
0	16.35	17.32	18.35	19.45	20.60	21.83	23.12	24.50	25.96	27.50	29.14	30.87
1	32.70	34.65	36.71	38.89	41.20	43.65	46.25	49.00	51.91	55.00	58.27	61.74
2	65.41	69.30	73.42	77.78	82.41	87.31	92.50	98.00	103.8	110.0	116.5	123.5
3	130.8	138.6	146.8	155.6	164.8	174.6	185.0	196.0	207.7	220.0	233.1	246.9
4	261.6	277.2	293.7	311.1	329.6	349.2	370.0	392.0	415.3	440.0	466.2	493.9
5	523.3	554.4	587.3	622.3	659.3	698.5	740.0	784.0	830.6	880.0	932.3	987.8
6	1047	1109	1175	1245	1319	1397	1480	1568	1661	1760	1865	1976
7	2093	2217	2349	2489	2637	2794	2960	3136	3322	3520	3729	3951
8	4186	4435	4699	4978	5274	5588	5920	6272	6645	7040	7459	7902

This chart is a KEY REFERENCE. The vertical numbers 0 through 8 represent octaves on the piano keyboard. The horizontal letters are the 12 notes, including sharps and flats. Every octave in ANY frequency is doubled from 0 to 1, 1 to 2, 2 to 3, etc. – all the way up to octave 8. This tells you that frequency relationships are exactingly precise in their relative sequence of preceding or descending order.

A note is either "higher" or "lower" in sound according to the relative vibrations in a twelve note octave categorical arrangement. Go down the line vertically for each note and see for yourself. The easiest example is to take A-0 through A-8. You'll notice that each set of frequencies doubles as it ascends up the octave range. It really doesn't get any more exacting than this. Music is a solid mathematical set of relationships between sonic frequencies. The higher the frequency, the higher the note.

Furthermore, frequencies within a given Major Key Signature resonate in mathematical symmetry with all the other notes within the scale. This occurs especially with octaves, major thirds, perfect fourths and perfect fifths – and, inverted fifths.

These relationships will be further clarified in Chapter 15, which will illustrate different drum kit configurations – along with all of the symmetrical relationships that occur when the kit is properly tuned.

Piano Keyboard/Frequency Chart

*Important Note: Drum FUNDAMENTAL NOTES generally range
from **F-1** (low) to **B-3** (high)
(Snare Batter & Reso heads are tuned one octave higher than their respective
fundamental notes)

Note name	Keyboard	Frequency Hz	
A0		27.500	
B0		30.868	29.135
C1		32.703	
D1		36.708	34.648
E1		41.203	38.891
F1		43.654	
G1		48.999	46.249
A1		55.000	51.913
B1		61.735	58.270
C2		65.406	
D2		73.416	69.296
E2		82.407	77.782
F2		87.307	
G2		97.999	92.499
A2		110.00	103.83
B2		123.47	116.54
C3		130.81	
D3		146.83	138.59
E3		164.81	155.56
F3		174.61	
G3		196.00	185.00
A3		220.00	207.65
B3		246.94	233.08
C4		**261.63**	
D4		293.67	277.18
E4		329.63	311.13
F4		349.23	
G4		392.00	369.99
A4		**440.00**	415.30
B4		493.88	466.16
C5		523.25	
D5		587.33	554.37
E5		659.26	622.25
F5		698.46	
G5		783.99	739.99
A5		880.00	830.61
B5		987.77	932.33
C6		1046.5	
D6		1174.7	1108.7
E6		1318.5	1244.5
F6		1396.9	
G6		1568.0	1480.0
A6		1760.0	1661.2
B6		1975.5	1864.7
C7		2093.0	
D7		2349.3	2217.5
E7		2637.0	2489.0
F7		2793.0	
G7		3136.0	2960.0
A7		3520.0	3322.4
B7		3951.1	3729.3

FUNDAMENTAL NOTES

Snare reso & batter tuning
Eb-4 to B-4

Bar Chart - Notes & Frequencies

The following **Chart** (see below) illustrates the most common FUNDAMENTAL NOTES ranging from 5" x 14" Snare drum to 16" x 22" Kick drum. In the vertical graph, the Snare is in the upper right, and the Kick is at the lower left. All other drums — ranging from 10" to 16" Toms in diameter fall in between according to their respective sizes. You will notice that the Dynamic Tuning Range from Kick to Snare is **F-1** (low) to **B-3** (high). The chart also shows how many of the shell sizes can overlap in tuning range. Whether or not one opts to use an electronic tuning device, this chart is highly valuable in determining which frequencies comfortably suit the dynamic range of a particular drum's shell size.

Note: *As mentioned earlier, dynamic tuning range is contingent more upon shell diameter than shell depth. This will be evident whether you're tuning an 8" x 12" tom, or a 16" x 16" floor tom. The principals of fourths work either way. Shell depth has more to do with the tonal elements of attack or decay. The shallower the depth, the more attack. The deeper the depth, the more decay. Therefore, when I use a 16" x 22" kick drum for example, the tuning capabilities don't change whether you have a 18" x 22" or a 14" x 24" kick drum.*

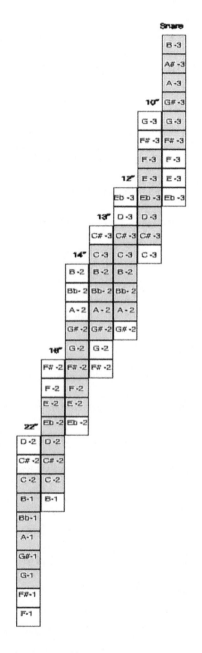

Chapter Fourteen

Putting It All Together

The possibilities of different drum tuning configurations are literally exponential. You already have the tools to arrive at any given drum's fundamental note. With all the information you now have on drum shell tuning ranges (based on size), I am providing eight tuning possibilities from which your drum set will be in perfect harmonic resonance as a complete instrument. If you are a drummer, a technician, or music producer who has a firm grasp on music theory, then the sky is the limit with what tuning potentials you can arrive at.

With the knowledge that I have provided for you, I encourage that you begin putting this to practice. Your drum kit can be easily designed in its tuning parameters to cover all styles of music. The notes, tuning frequencies -- and their powerful relationships **that you're about to find out with kit examples** -- will enable anyone the skills to tune their drums to any genre: jazz, rock, latin, swing, or whatever best suits your needs.

Furthermore, you may easily discover that one or two basic tuning set ups for your kit may adapt perfectly well to any genre of music (The Key of **C** – **Major** being perhaps the most universal). The following examples are presented only in the eight **major** scales -- with *different* tuning possibilities in each scale. With the many different scale possibilities in music, drum kit tuning potentials are practically limitless.

Chapter Fifteen

8 Tuning Diagrams Based on
4 Drum Kit Configurations

In the following pages, I am providing 8 diagrams of basic kit configurations. Each configuration will show two tuning possibilities from which each **drum kit** will be a complete instrument tuned in harmonic balance. The set ups are as follows:

1. 4 Piece Kit -- Two examples
2. 5 Piece Kit (2 Up, and 1 Down) - Two examples
3. 5 Piece Kit (1 Up, and 2 Down) - Two examples
4. 6 Piece Kit (2 Up, and 2 Down) - Two examples

As a complete kit/instrument, you will notice that all drums in the following examples are in tune with each other. Each kit will resonate in complete harmony with itself. Some of the examples have already been established as drum tuning standards. Yet, this book can now tell you exactly HOW to arrive at such standards as well as create innumerable others -- including potential *new standards*.

Understand that, by the very nature of tuning each drum in perfect 4ths (with reso head being tuned a 4th higher than the batter head), a host of musical relationships flood your tuning capabilities for the entire kit. There are vast possibilities. The following 8 configurations will give you just a few ideas. You'll see that as configurations increase, so do the musical relations among all drums.

4 Piece Kit

C - Major

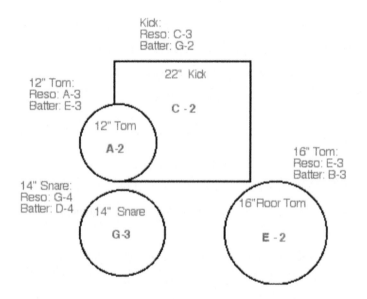

Kick:
Reso: C-3
Batter: G-2

22" Kick

C - 2

12" Tom:
Reso: A-3
Batter: E-3

12" Tom

A-2

16" Tom:
Reso: E-3
Batter: B-3

14" Snare:
Reso: G-4
Batter: D-4

14" Snare

G-3

16"Floor Tom

E - 2

4 Piece Kit
C - Major

*Note: Compare Diagram (left) with Musical Relationships throughout entire kit (below):

Snare Batter (D) and Kick batter (G) are a perfect 4th

Snare reso (G) and Kick batter (G) are two octaves apart

Snare reso (G) and Kick reso (C) are a perfect 4th

12" Tom batter (E) and 16" Tom batter (B) are a perfect 5th

12" Tom reso (A) and 16" Tom reso (E) are a perfect 5th

12" Tom reso (A) and Snare batter (D) are a perfect 4th

16" Tom reso (E) and 12" Tom reso (A) are a perfect 4th

Kick reso (C) and 16" reso (E) are a major 3rd

Kick reso (C) and 12" Tom batter (E) are a major 3rd

4 Piece Kit

D - Major

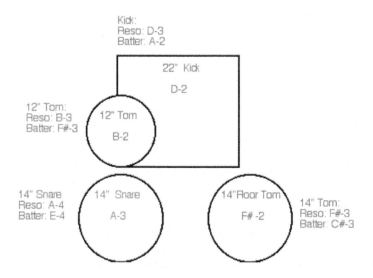

Kick:
Reso: D-3
Batter: A-2

22" Kick

D-2

12" Tom:
Reso: B-3
Batter: F#-3

12" Tom

B-2

14" Snare
Reso: A-4
Batter: E-4

14" Snare

A-3

14" Floor Tom

F# -2

14" Tom:
Reso: F#-3
Batter: C#-3

4 Piece Kit
D - Major

*Note: Compare Diagram (left) with Musical Relationships throughout entire kit (below):

Snare batter (E) and 12" Tom reso (B) are a perfect 5th

Snare batter (E) and Kick batter (A) are a perfect 4th

Snare reso (A) and Kick reso (D) are a perfect 4th

Snare reso (A) and 14" Tom batter (C#) are a major 3rd

12" Tom batter (F#) and 14" Tom batter (C#) are a perfect 5th

12" Tom batter (F#) and 14" Tom reso (F#) are in perfect pitch

Kick reso (D) and 14" Tom reso (F#) are a major 3rd

Kick batter (A) and Snare reso (A) are two octaves apart

Kick batter (A) and Snare batter (E) are a perfect 5th

5 Piece Kit – 2 up 1 down

A - Major

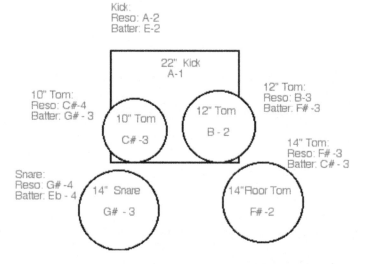

Kick:
Reso: A-2
Batter: E-2

22" Kick
A-1

10" Tom:
Reso: C#-4
Batter: G# - 3

10" Tom
C# -3

12" Tom
B - 2

12" Tom:
Reso: B-3
Batter: F# -3

14" Tom:
Reso: F# -3
Batter: C# - 3

Snare:
Reso: G# -4
Batter: Eb - 4

14" Snare
G# - 3

14"Floor Tom
F# -2

5 Piece Kit – 2 up 1 down
A - Major

*Note: Compare Diagram (left) with Musical Relationships throughout entire kit (below):

Snare reso (G#) and 10" Tom reso (C#) are a perfect 4th

Snare batter (Eb) and 10" Tom batter (G#) are a perfect 4th

10" Tom reso (C#) and 14" Tom reso (F#) are a perfect 4th

10" Tom reso (C#) and 14" batter (C#) are an octave apart

12" Tom reso (B) and 14" Tom reso (F#) are a perfect 5th

12" Tom batter (F#) and 14" Tom batter (C#) are a perfect 5th

12" Tom reso (B) and Kick batter (E) are perfect 4th

Kick batter (E) and Snare reso (G#) are a major 3rd

Kick reso (A) and 10" Tom reso (C#) are a major 3rd

Kick reso (A) and 14" Tom batter (C#) are a major 3rd

Kick batter (E) and 10" Tom batter (G#) are a major 3rd

Kick batter (E) and Snare Reso (G#) are a major 3rd

5 Piece Kit – 2 up 1 down

F - Major

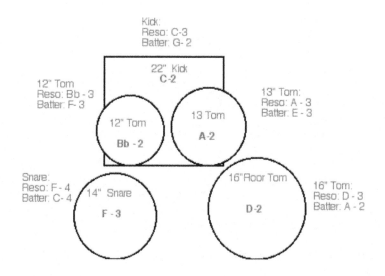

Kick:
Reso: C-3
Batter: G- 2

22" Kick
C-2

12" Tom
Reso: Bb - 3
Batter: F- 3

12" Tom
Bb - 2

13 Tom
A-2

13" Tom:
Reso: A - 3
Batter: E - 3

Snare:
Reso: F - 4
Batter: C- 4

14" Snare
F - 3

16"Floor Tom
D-2

16" Tom:
Reso: D - 3
Batter: A - 2

5 Piece Kit – 2 up 1 down
F - Major

*Note: Compare Diagram (left) with Musical Relationships throughout entire kit (below):

Snare reso (F) and 12" Tom reso (Bb) are a perfect 4th

Snare reso (F) and 12" Tom batter (F) are an octave apart

Snare batter (C) and Kick batter (G) are a perfect 5th

Snare batter (C) and 12" Tom batter (F) are a perfect 4th

12" Tom reso (Bb) and 16" Tom reso (D) are a major 3rd

12" Tom batter (F) and 16" Tom batter (A) are a major 3rd

13" Tom reso (A) and 16" Tom batter (A) are an octave apart

13" Tom reso (A) and 16" Tom reso (D) are a perfect 4th

16" Tom reso (D) and Kick batter (G) are a perfect 4th

Kick reso (C) and Snare reso (F) are a perfect 4th

Kick reso (C) and Snare batter (C) are an octave apart

5 Piece Kit – 1 up 2 down

E - Major

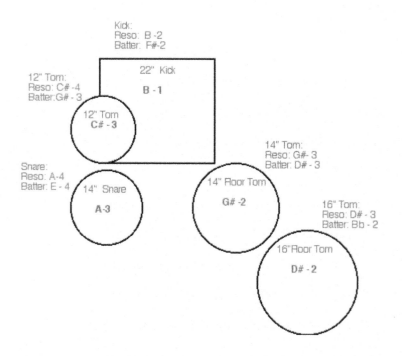

Kick:
Reso: B -2
Batter: F#-2

22" Kick
B - 1

12" Tom:
Reso: C# -4
Batter:G# - 3

12" Tom
C# - 3

14" Tom:
Reso: G#- 3
Batter: D# - 3

14" Floor Tom
G# -2

Snare:
Reso: A-4
Batter: E - 4

14" Snare
A-3

16" Tom:
Reso: D# - 3
Batter: Bb - 2

16"Floor Tom
D# - 2

5 Piece Kit – 1 up 2 down
E - Major

*Note: Compare Diagram (left) with Musical Relationships throughout entire kit (below):

Snare reso (A) and 12" Tom reso (C#) are a major 3rd

Snare batter (E) and 12" Tom batter (G#) are a major 3rd

Snare batter (E) and Kick reso (B) are a perfect 5th

12" Tom reso (C#) and 14" Tom reso (G#) are a perfect 5th

12" Tom reso (C#) and Kick batter (F#) are a perfect 4th

14" Tom batter (D#) and 12" Tom batter (G#) are a perfect 4th

14" Tom reso (G#) and 16" Tom reso (D#) are a perfect 5th

16" Tom batter (Bb) and 14" Tom batter (D#) are a perfect 4th

Kick reso (B) and 14" Tom batter (D#) are a major 3rd

Kick reso (B) and 16" Tom reso (D#) are a major 3rd

Kick reso (B) and Snare batter (E) are a perfect 4th

5 Piece Kit – 1 up 2 down

G - Major

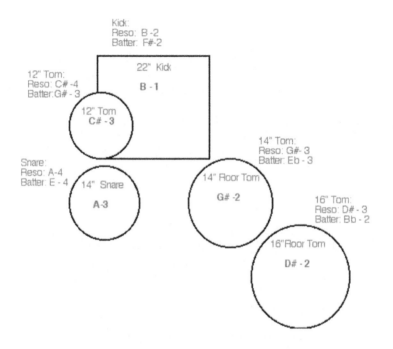

Kick:
Reso: B -2
Batter: F#-2

22" Kick

B - 1

12" Tom:
Reso: C# -4
Batter:G# - 3

12" Tom
C# - 3

14" Tom:
Reso: G#- 3
Batter: Eb - 3

Snare:
Reso: A-4
Batter: E - 4

14" Snare

A-3

14" Floor Tom

G# -2

16" Tom:
Reso: D#- 3
Batter: Bb - 2

16"Floor Tom

D# - 2

5 Piece Kit – 1 up 2 down
G - Major

*Note: Compare Diagram (left) with Musical Relationships throughout entire kit (below):

Snare reso (A) and 14" Tom batter (D) are a perfect 4th

Snare reso (A) an 16" Tom reso (D) are a perfect 4th

Snare reso (A) and 16" Tom batter (A) are two octaves apart

13" Tom reso (C)and Kick batter(G) are a perfect 5th

13" Tom reso (C) and 14" Tom reso (G) are a perfect 5th

13" Tom batter (G) and Kick batter (G) are an octave apart

13" Tom batter (G) and 14" Tom batter (D) are a perfect 5th

13" Tom batter (G) and 16" Tom reso (D) are a perfect 5th

14" Tom reso (G) and 16" Tom reso (D) are a perfect 5th

14" Tom batter (D) and 16" Tom batter (A) are a perfect 5th

14" Tom batter (D) and 16" Tom reso (D) are in perfect pitch

Kick batter (G) and 16" Tom reso (D) are a perfect 5th

Kick reso (C) and 14" reso (G) are a perfect 5th

6 Piece Kit – 2 up 2 down

B - Major

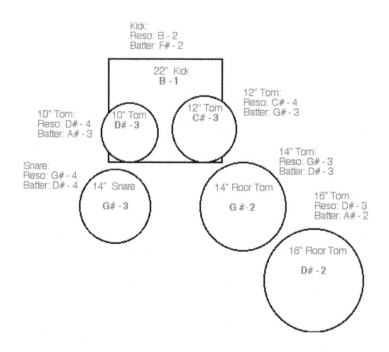

Kick:
Reso: B - 2
Batter: F# - 2

22" Kick
B - 1

12" Tom:
Reso: C# - 4
Batter: G# - 3

10" Tom:
Reso: D# - 4
Batter: A# - 3

10" Tom
D# - 3

12" Tom
C# - 3

14" Tom:
Reso: G# - 3
Batter: D# - 3

Snare:
Reso: G# - 4
Batter: D# - 4

14" Snare
G# - 3

14" Floor Tom
G #- 2

16" Tom:
Reso: D# - 3
Batter: A# - 2

16" Floor Tom
D# - 2

6 Piece Kit – 2 up 2 down
B - Major

*Note: Compare Diagram (left) with Musical Relationships throughout entire kit (below):

Snare reso (G#) and 10" Tom reso (D#) are a perfect 5th
Snare reso (G#) and 12" Tom reso (C#) are a perfect 4th
Snare reso (G#) and 14" Tom batter (D#) are a perfect 5th
Snare reso (G#) and 16" Tom reso (D#) are a perfect 5th
Snare batter (D#) and 10" Tom reso (D#) are in perfect pitch
Snare batter (D#) and 12" Tom batter (G#) are a perfect 4th
Snare batter (D#) and 14" Tom reso (G#) are a perfect 4th
Snare batter (D#) and 10" Tom batter (A#) are a perfect 5th
Snare batter (D#) and 14" Tom batter (D#) are an octave apart
Snare batter (D#) and 16" Tom Reso (D#) are an octave apart
10" Tom reso (D#) and 12" Tom batter (G#) are a perfect 4th
10" Tom reso (D#) and 14" Tom reso (G#) are a perfect 4th
10" Tom reso (D#) and 16" Tom reso (D#) are an octave apart
12" Tom reso (C#) and 14" Tom reso (G#) are a perfect 5th
14" Tom reso (G#) and 16" Tom reso (D#) are a perfect 5th
14" Tom batter (D#) and 16" Tom reso (D#) in perfect pitch
14" Tom batter (D#) and 16" Tom batter (A#) are a perfect 5th
Kick reso (B) and Snare batter (D#) are a major 3rd
Kick reso (B) and 10" Tom reso (D#) are a major 3rd
Kick reso (B) and 14" Tom batter (D#) are a major 3rd
Kick reso (B) and 16" Tom reso (D#) are a major 3rd
Kick batter (F#) and 10" Tom batter (A#) are a major 3rd
Kick batter (F#) and 16" Tom batter (A#) are a major 3rd
Kick batter (F#) and 12" Tom reso (C#) are a perfect 5th

6 Piece Kit – 2 up 2 down

F# - Major

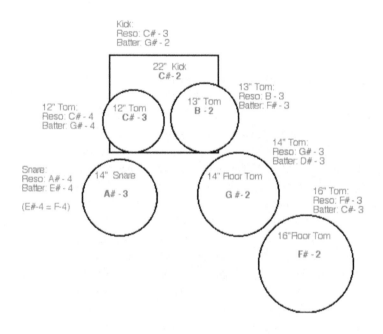

Kick:
Reso: C# - 3
Batter: G# - 2

22" Kick
C#- 2

13" Tom:
Reso: B - 3
Batter: F# - 3

12" Tom:
Reso: C# - 4
Batter: G# - 4

12" Tom
C# - 3

13" Tom
B - 2

14" Tom:
Reso: G# - 3
Batter: D# - 3

Snare:
Reso: A# - 4
Batter: E# - 4

(E#-4 = F-4)

14" Snare
A# - 3

14" Floor Tom
G #- 2

16" Tom:
Reso: F# - 3
Batter: C#- 3

16"Floor Tom
F# - 2

6 Piece Kit – 2 up 2 down

F# - Major

*Note: Compare Diagram (left) with Musical Relationships throughout entire kit (below):

Snare reso (A#) and 14" Tom batter (D#) are a perfect 4th
12" Tom reso (C#) and 13" Tom batter (F#) are a perfect 4th
12" Tom reso (C#) and14" Tom reso (G#) are a perfect 5th
12" Tom reso (C#) and 16" Tom reso (F#) are a perfect 4th
12" Tom reso (C#) and 16" Tom batter (C#) one octave apart
12" Tom reso (C#) and Kick reso (C#) are an octave apart
12" Tom batter (G#) and 14" batter (D#) are a perfect 5th
12" Tom batter (G#) and 16" Tom batter (C#) are a perfect 4th
12" Tom batter (G#) and 14" Tom reso (G#) one octave apart
12" Tom batter (G#) and Kick batter (G#) two octaves apart
13" Tom reso (B) and 14" Tom batter (D#) are a major 3rd
13" Tom reso (B) and 16" Tom reso (F#) are a perfect 5th
13" Tom batter (F#) and Snare reso (A#) are a major 3rd
13" Tom batter (F#) and 12" Tom reso (C#) are a perfect 5th
13" Tom batter (F#) and 16" batter (C#) are a perfect 5th
13" Tom batter (F#) and Kick reso (C#) are a perfect 5th
14" Tom reso (G#) and 12" Tom reso (C#) are a perfect 4th
14" Tom reso (G#) and 16" Tom batter (C#) are a perfect 4th
14" Tom reso (G#) and Kick batter (G#) are an octave apart
16" Tom reso (F#) and Snare reso (A#) are a major 3rd
Kick reso (C#) and 16" Tom batter (C#) are in perfect pitch
Kick batter (G#) and 14" Tom batter (D#) are a perfect 5th
Kick batter (G#) and 14" reso (G#) are an octave apart

Conclusion

Y ou have just seen in our last two diagrams showing 6 piece kits in the keys of B Major, and F# Major that there are over twenty three harmonic relationships among all drums — in each example! This isn't to mention inverted 4ths and 5ths which I didn't list. As you can clearly see, there is amazing potential to tuning any drum kit with complete musical precision. The more musical your drums are, the better they will sound. This precision is derived from the very basic formulas I have presented in this book. The key is determining a Fundamental Note in the resonant head when pitched a perfect fourth higher than the batter head.

All of the basic samples that I have illustrated and listed in the previous 8 drum configuration diagrams show these various relationships between and among all the drums that comprise the kit. When musically tuned according to the major scales alone, the harmonic resonant activity ping pongs throughout the entire kit -- from resonant and batter heads – relating to one another in either perfect pitch, octaves, or perfect 3rds, 4ths, and 5ths.

Furthermore, the tuning examples I have provided are realistic in terms of emulating conventional approaches to drum tuning in configurations used by drummers worldwide. Only now, it's no longer a hit or miss proposition. You have complete command over *exactly* how you want your drums, and drum kit to sound. It is from this method from which you may accomplish such control.

As a complete instrument, the drum kit resonates with itself in perfect union. Unrelated overtones are virtually diminished. The clarity of overall sound quality produced by a cohesively tuned set of drums delivers unparalleled tonal response. Tuning your drums no longer has to be a mystery. Not only can a drummer express his or her own personality into how they go about tuning, but they now have access to a method that makes complete musical sense around the board.

I sincerely wish that you take the brief amount of time to become completely   familiar and incorporate this tuning method into your drumming arsenal. As mentioned, use of tuning devices is welcome. Yet, it isn't the gadget that tunes your drums. You do. Frequency finding devices can be helpful in allowing you to fine tune your drums by offering feedback. But, they don't show you how to deliberately select the notes that you specifically desire -- especially in a relationship of fourths that broaden harmonic resonance and tonal symmetry.

This method that I have devised, practiced, and have now shared with you can open untold potential to how you want to create your own drum sound. Since there has been no real overall established convention in drum tuning, I can only hope that my love and passion for drumming may enable all drummers to realize that there does actually exist a technique and method in drum tuning that is easy to follow, and produces absolute consistent results with no guess work.

Epilogue

In the early to mid eighteenth century, Johann Sebastian Bach wrote two books of preludes and fugues in all 24 major and minor keys. These two works have been since comprised as one single work called *The Well-Tempered Clavier*, or *The 48*. Bach's initial intention was to arrive at equal *temperament*, or tuning, of each of these musical works. His purpose was to represent a musical equation of the most tonally arranged keys. Bach would tune his own harpsichords and clavichords to accomplish this since he found standard tunings as being unsatisfactory.

Since music involves relative mathematical ratios of frequency vibrations, Bach wanted to eliminate the unwanted frequencies that clashed from notes that resonated from standard tunings. He kept things simple as to avoid what was termed as "accidentals." Bach well understood that the fourth and fifth intervals are known as perfect because they stay in the major key when inverted.

It is by no accident that what I've stumbled upon in my method of drum tuning, which is based on the relationship of perfect 4^{ths} (or, inverted 5^{ths}), keeps everything in *perfect temperament* with all of the other tuned drums in a specific key.

I have always relied upon my ears to guide how I've tuned. However, my diligent experimentation with the drum tuning process has led me to discover what I have now laid forth in this book. It wasn't until a dear friend, and professional violinist, read my first draft of this book and informed me of how closely my method is in alignment with Bach's *Well-Tempered Clavier* approach to tuning.

This noted fact in musical history alone reinforces that all that I have shared in this method falls well under the fundamental laws of music dynamics and the exacting relationships that can be calculated in relative harmonic frequencies. In honor of Bach's amazing contribution to music, musicians, and music appreciation, I call this method *The Well-Tempered Drum Kit.*

About the Author

George Kiapos' creative professional career has spanned as an Architect/Builder, musician, inventor, writer and international artist. A Los Angeles native, he has taken his design and building expertise into both drum, and acoustic guitar making. He has always sought out to examine the finest details as to how things are put together, and -- more importantly -- how they work best. His knowledge of acoustic instrument building and design has inspired him to get to the root of understanding the tonal characteristics and possibilities that are necessary for producing an instrument's greatest potential. He understands that the tuning and intonation of any instrument plays a critical role in its overall performance. Since no musical convention has been established for drum kit tuning, years of research studying the acoustical dynamics of drums had found him determined to devise a method that can always be relied upon with unfailing consistency. *The Well-Tempered Drum Kit Method* is now the solution.

Made in the USA
Monee, IL
23 May 2023

34379229R00042